MODERN ENGINEERING MARVELS

SELF-DRIVING CARS

Christine Zuchora-Walske

**Checkerboard
Library**

An Imprint of Abdo Publishing
abdopublishing.com

ABDOPUBLISHING.COM

Published by Abdo Publishing, a division of ABDO, PO Box 398166, Minneapolis, Minnesota 55439.
Copyright © 2018 by Abdo Consulting Group, Inc. International copyrights reserved in all countries.
No part of this book may be reproduced in any form without written permission from the publisher.
Checkerboard Library™ is a trademark and logo of Abdo Publishing.

Printed in the United States of America, North Mankato, Minnesota
062017
092017

 THIS BOOK CONTAINS
RECYCLED MATERIALS

Design: Kelly Doudna, Mighty Media, Inc.
Production: Mighty Media, Inc.
Editor: Liz Salzmann
Cover Photograph: AP Images
Interior Photographs: AP Images, pp. 1, 19, 21, 23, 25, 26, 29 (top), 29 (bottom); Shutterstock, pp.
5, 6, 7, 10, 11, 14, 15, 22, 27, 28 (bottom left), 28 (bottom right); Wikimedia Commons, pp. 13, 17;
William Creswell/Wikimedia Commons, pp. 9, 28 (top)

Publisher's Cataloging-in-Publication Data

Names: Zuchora-Walske, Christine, author.
Title: Self-driving cars / by Christine Zuchora-Walske.
Description: Minneapolis, MN : Abdo Publishing, 2018. | Series: Modern
    engineering marvels.
Identifiers: LCCN 2016962795 | ISBN 9781532110900 (lib. bdg.) |
    ISBN 9781680788754 (ebook)
Subjects: LCSH: Automobiles--technological innovations--Juvenile literature. |
    Technological innovations--Juvenile literature. | Inventions--Juvenile
    literature.
Classification: DDC 600--dc23
LC record available at http://lccn.loc.gov/2016962795

CONTENTS

SELF-DRIVING CARS OF THE FUTURE

1

It's 7:30 am. A small, round car rolls to a stop in front of your home. You and your big sister hop into the car. You wave to your dad. He's standing in the doorway, waving back. The car has no driver. But it knows where to go.

You are in a self-driving car! Your parents pay for this service. A car picks you up every weekday morning. It takes you to middle school. Then it takes your sister to high school. After school, it picks you both up and brings you home.

The car is clean, quiet, and comfortable. There are no controls except an emergency button. You can push it in case something goes terribly wrong. This will stop the car and call for help. But you have never needed to push the button.

You pass a tree-lined playground. Your dad says it used to be a parking lot. Now that most people use self-driving car services, there are fewer cars and fewer parking lots. There is also less pollution. Your dad likes that.

The whole interior of a car could change with self-driving cars. With seats facing each other, families could talk and interact much more easily!

When your dad was a kid, people drove their own cars most of the time. He says it feels strange to ride in cars with no drivers. But you've been riding in self-driving cars all your life. It's normal for you.

A world of self-driving cars may seem like a wild dream. But these cars already exist! Engineers are working on making them safe for everyone to use. This is just the latest chapter in the story of automobiles. That story began more than 300 years ago.

In the 1600s, French scientist Denis Papin experimented with steam. He realized he could use steam to move things. He put water and a piston in a tube. Papin heated the water, creating steam. The steam moved the piston up and down.

Other scientists used Papin's idea to invent the steam engine. The first steam engines were used in coal mines to pump water out of the ground. Then, in the 1770s, British engineers James Watt and Matthew Boulton invented a new kind of steam engine. It was called a **rotary** engine.

TECH TIDBIT

A piston is a **cylinder** attached to a rod. The piston moves up and down. This lets the rod turn a machine part.

Most trains stopped using steam engines by the 1950s. But some steam engines are still used on tourist and heritage lines.

Rotary engines led to major advancements in transportation. These engines could spin wheels and **propellers**. Wheels and propellers could move **vehicles**. People started putting rotary steam engines in trains, boats, tractors, and automobiles.

The demand for automobiles, or cars, grew quickly. By 1900, gasoline engines were replacing steam engines. Gasoline-powered cars were safer and easier to control than steam cars. Steam car boilers sometimes exploded.

At first, cars were expensive. Only wealthy people could afford them. But by the 1920s, cars were cheap enough for ordinary people. This was mostly due to the introduction of assembly lines. Assembly lines reduced the time and cost needed to build cars. So, car companies could charge buyers less.

Cars grew more and more popular over the next century. Car makers kept improving their cars. They made changes for comfort, safety, and easier driving.

For example, they added roofs and windows to protect riders. Heaters kept people warm on cold days. Better brakes could stop a car more quickly and smoothly. But these changes were just the beginning. People continued to look for new ways to make better cars.

The Ford Model T was the first affordable car in the United States. More than 15 million Model Ts were built from 1913 to 1927.

Ever since cars hit the road, they have helped people. They make travel fast, comfortable, and easy. Many people prefer driving cars to walking, biking, or riding buses and trains.

But cars have drawbacks. They're costly to buy, fix, and fuel. Car exhaust is bad for the **environment**. And cars are dangerous. When car accidents happen, people can be hurt or killed.

Safety has always been a problem for cars. In the early 1900s, the number of cars increased quickly. At first people didn't know how to deal with all those cars. Driver training didn't exist. Neither did road signs, stoplights, or lane lines. Many accidents happened.

This led people to start dreaming of self-driving cars. They thought such cars could be safer, faster, and

TECH TIDBIT

Detroit, Michigan, police officer William Potts invented the three-color traffic light in 1920.

Cars are the most popular mode of transportation. There are an estimated 1.2 billion motor vehicles in the world!

easier to use. But to travel the roads safely, cars need "brains" to guide them. These brains can be human or computer. Computer **technology** did not exist when cars were invented. So, every car had to have a person driving it.

5 COMPUTERS TO THE RESCUE

The first computers were invented in the 1930s. These early computers were huge. One computer could fill an entire room! And early computers were designed to work on one type of problem or calculation.

But in the 1960s, computer science started advancing quickly. Computers became smaller and more reliable. They also got more powerful. They could do many **complex** tasks. For example, computers began guiding **missiles**. Computers at that time could also fly airplanes and control robots.

With better computers, the dream of self-driving cars seemed more possible. Engineers started working toward it. They identified three key tasks a self-driving car's computer would need to do:

- sense the car's surroundings
- recognize objects and make decisions about them
- tell the car how to react to its surroundings

One early computer was the AVIDAC. The Argonne National Laboratory in Illinois completed it in 1953.

After identifying these important tasks, engineers started working to invent cars that could do them. An early example of a driverless car was the Stanford Cart. Scientists at Stanford University in California created it in the 1960s.

This cart was a **vehicle** that could be operated by remote control. The cart sent video images of its surroundings to a remote operator. The operator used the images to see where to drive the cart. But the video transmission was slow, so the cart could only go five mph (8 kmh).

More advancements came in the 1980s and 1990s. In 1987, many European universities and car makers joined the Eureka PROMETHEUS project. The project's goal was to improve traffic safety. Part of the project was developing driverless cars. Computerized research vehicles in Germany and Italy drove thousands of miles with little human help. The project ended in 1995.

Computers and **technology** continued to improve. This has led to cars slowly becoming more and more **automated**. Today, many regular cars contain some self-driving features. These include:

TECH TIDBIT

The integrated circuit (IC) was invented in 1958. ICs were small devices used in computers to hold data. With ICs, computers could be a lot smaller.

- Adaptive **cruise control** keeps a moving car a safe distance away from the car ahead of it.
- Anti-lock brake systems keep wheels from locking. This prevents skidding and makes it easier and safer to stop quickly.

The Infiniti Q50 uses cameras and sensors to warn the driver of possible collisions.

- Electronic stability control prevents skidding and spinning out when a driver turns the steering wheel too hard or not hard enough.
- Emergency braking stops a car when it's about to hit something.
- Lane keeping gently steers a drifting car back into its driving lane.
- Self-parking steers a car into a parking spot.

While cars have become more **automated**, the search for a completely driverless car has continued. This effort got a boost from the US Department of Defense (DOD) in 2002. The DOD announced that its Defense Advanced Research Projects Agency (DARPA) was holding a contest. The contest was called the DARPA Grand Challenge.

The entrants had two years to design driverless cars that could navigate a 142-mile (228 km) route. The first **vehicle** that finished the course would win $1 million. Fifteen vehicles were entered in the contest. They raced in March 2004. However, none of the cars could complete the course.

Even so, the race was a success. It brought scientists, students, inventors, racers, mechanics, and dreamers together to solve a tricky problem. The ideas they brought to the contest sparked an explosion of research on self-driving cars.

DARPA held another Grand Challenge in 2005. This time, the top prize was $2 million and 195 teams entered. Five vehicles

Self-driving vehicle TerraMax navigates the 2005 DARPA Grand Challenge route. TerraMax was built by a team led by Wisconsin company Oshkosh Defense.

finished. The winner was Stanley, a **vehicle** designed by a team from Stanford University. Stanley finished in about seven hours.

Stanley had several features that helped it win. For example, Stanley had not only a **Global Positioning System (GPS)**, but also a camera and **lidar** and **radar** sensors. The camera and sensors let Stanley actually "see" its surroundings. Also, Stanley's computer could learn from its mistakes. At first, it thought shadows were obstacles. But eventually, Stanley learned that it could drive through shadows.

The first Grand Challenges were held in the desert. DARPA held a third Grand Challenge in 2007. This one was called the DARPA **Urban** Challenge. In it, the cars drove 60 miles (96 km) of city streets in Victorville, California.

The cars had to follow a route, obey traffic laws, and interact with other cars. Eleven teams entered the race. Six finished. The $2 million winner was Boss, a car designed by a team from Carnegie Mellon University in Pittsburgh, Pennsylvania.

Boss won because of two big advantages: tough testing and a clever computer. Boss's team ran more than 2,000 miles (3,219 km) of test runs. During each run, its computer created an **animation** of what Boss saw and did. The team watched the animation to understand Boss's reactions. This helped the team spot and fix problems quickly.

The DARPA races spurred research at many universities and car makers. This led to better sensors. With better sensors,

SEBASTIAN THRUN

Sebastian Thrun was born in Germany in 1967. He studied **robotics** in college. After college, Thrun invented robotic guides for museums. The robots led tours and explained exhibits to visitors.

These robots got Stanford University's attention. In 2004, Stanford invited Thrun to head its robotics laboratory. Thrun led the teams for both self-driving vehicles Stanley and Junior (2007 **Urban** Challenge second-place finisher).

Technology company Google was impressed with Thrun's work. It hired Thrun to lead its self-driving car project. Through Thrun's work, he became known as the father of self-driving cars.

Sebastian Thrun with self-driving car Stanley

self-driving cars could see and interpret their surroundings more clearly. It also led to better computer programs for following roads and avoiding crashes.

SELF-DRIVING CARS AT WORK

Self-driving **vehicles** are currently being used in closed locations. These are specific areas that the vehicles operate in. Closed locations include farms, resorts, **campuses**, and factories.

Self-driving farm tractors have been used since the early 2000s. They can run with or without human help. For example, some farmers let their tractors drive themselves along straight rows, but take over to turn corners. Other farmers program their tractors to travel an entire field with no human driving help at all.

Self-driving cars can carry people within places such as resorts, airports, and college campuses. Navya is a French company that has been making self-driving minibuses for this type of use since 2015.

Canadian company Clearpath **Robotics** makes driverless vehicles for factories and warehouses. They move supplies around these huge buildings. Machinery manufacturers Caterpillar and John Deere both use Clearpath products.

A Navya self-driving bus carries visitors through the Park of the Gardens in Bad Zwischenahn, Germany.

It is more challenging to make driverless cars that can navigate streets and highways. These cars have to be able to detect and respond to many more different situations. Despite the difficulties, there are some **vehicles** with self-driving **technology** on the road today.

In 2016, car service company Uber started testing completely self-driving cars in Pittsburgh, Pennsylvania. The cars are made by car manufacturer Volvo. Uber customers there can be picked up by one of Uber's robo-taxis. The cars use cameras, **GPS**, **lidar** and **radar** sensors, and computers to operate the controls and navigate routes.

TECH TIDBIT

An airplane's **autopilot** system uses radar and other technology similar to that used in self-driving cars.

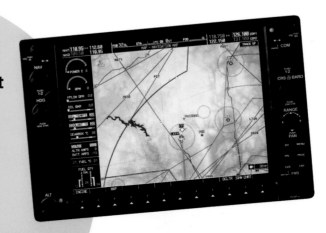

During the testing stage, Uber customers can refuse to ride in a robo-taxi. But, if a rider accepts, he or she gets to ride for free!

Early users say they feel safe and get where they need to go. However, a robo-taxi is a bit slower than a taxi with a human driver. For now, an Uber employee rides in each robo-taxi as a backup. But Uber's goal is to eventually use cars with no drivers at all.

9 RIDING INTO THE FUTURE

Driverless cars are only in the early stages of development. But there are constant improvements. The more miles self-driving cars travel, the more their computers learn about driving. Meanwhile, engineers learn how to program the computers better. As a result, cars get better at driving safely.

Two companies are leading the way in driverless car **technology**. These companies are Google and Tesla. Both of them are working hard to learn as much as possible through testing self-driving cars on the road.

Google, with manufacturing help from car makers, has built test cars that are fully self-driving. In total, these cars have traveled more than 2 million miles (3,218,688 km). There have only been a few minor accidents. Engineers adjust Google's cars to improve performance. The cars learn to sense and react to nearly anything. Google is developing cars meant for driving services such as Uber. It hopes to have cars for driving services ready by 2019.

All Tesla cars are now equipped with 8 cameras and 12 sensors. The system can see in every direction at once and far beyond human abilities!

Tesla is taking a different approach. It's building **optional** self-driving **technology** into all of its cars. This way, all Tesla drivers can test the technology if they choose. Teslas have traveled more than 130 million miles (209 million km) in self-driving mode. However, the **technology** still requires human supervision. In May 2016, one person died while riding in a Tesla that was driving itself.

Self-driving car makers have to deal with a lot of uncertainty in terms of laws. They have to navigate different rules of the road in every US state. But the US federal government is starting to create nationwide laws. In September 2016, it released its first rule book for self-driving cars. The rules require car companies to share information about their technology with the government. This will help the government study how self-driving cars perform on the road.

Nobody really knows what the future holds for self-driving cars. And it's not just about the cars themselves. People's attitudes about transportation will have to change to make driverless cars part of everyday life.

Google's self-driving car program will be called Waymo. This is short for "a new way forward in mobility."

GOOGLE CAR

LIDAR
Lidar sensors detect objects in every direction.

BATTERY
A powerful battery stores electricity for the car's engine.

INSIDE
An orientation sensor tracks motion and balance.

SHAPE
A rounded shape helps the sensors see as much as possible.

RADAR
Radar sensors monitor the speed of **vehicles** ahead.

WHEEL SENSORS
Wheel sensors detect rotation and help the car know where it is.

COMPUTER
The computer receives input from all of the sensors. Then it makes decisions and tells the car what to do.

TECH TIMELINE

1770s

James Watt and Matthew Boulton invent the rotary steam engine.

1920s

Cars become cheap enough for ordinary people to afford.

1600s

Denis Papin builds a steam cooker, then uses what he learns to build a steam-powered piston.

1930s

The first computers are invented.

1958

Jack Kilby and Robert Noyce invent the integrated circuit (IC).

1987–1995

European engineers join the Eureka PROMETHEUS project to develop self-driving car technology.

2005

Stanford University's Stanley wins the second DARPA Grand Challenge.

1960s

Stanford University scientists develop the Stanford Cart.

2007

Carnegie Mellon University's Boss wins the DARPA Urban Challenge.

2016

Uber launches self-driving taxis in Pittsburgh.

GLOSSARY

animation–a scene or movie made up of a series of drawings, computer graphics, or photographs that appear to move due to slight changes in each image.

automated–able to move or act by itself.

autopilot–a system for automatically steering ships, aircraft, and spacecraft.

campus–the grounds and buildings of a school.

complex–having many parts, details, ideas, or functions.

cruise control–a device in a vehicle that keeps it going at a constant speed.

cylinder–a solid bounded by two parallel circles and a curved surface. A soda can is an example of a cylinder.

environment–all the surroundings that affect the growth and well-being of a living thing.

Global Positioning System (GPS)–a space-based navigation system used to pinpoint locations on Earth.

lidar–an instrument that uses pulses of laser light to detect and track objects.

missile–a weapon that is thrown or projected to hit a target.

optional–left to one's choice rather than required.

propeller–a device that has a revolving central part with blades. The spinning blades move a vehicle, such as a boat or an airplane.

radar–an instrument that uses the reflection of radio waves to detect and track objects.

robotics–technology that is used to design, build, and operate robots.

rotary–turning on an axis like a wheel.

technology–a capability given by the practical application of knowledge.

urban–of or relating to a city.

vehicle–something used to carry or transport. Cars, trucks, airplanes, and boats are vehicles.

WEBSITES

To learn more about Modern Engineering Marvels, visit **abdobooklinks.com**. These links are routinely monitored and updated to provide the most current information available.

INDEX